I0877676

FAMOUS ATHLETES

LEGENDS AND GAME CHANGERS

BY MELISSA ROSS

eureka!

eureka!

Eureka! books turn real stories into unforgettable experiences. This nonfiction imprint sparks curiosity, encourages critical thinking, and engages middle-grade readers. *Eureka!* books empower young minds to explore the stories of the real world, one fascinating fact at a time. Unravel the power of knowledge and lifelong learning with *Eureka!*

This edition first published in 2026 by Bellwether Media, Inc.

No part of this publication may be reproduced in whole or in part without written permission of the publisher. For information regarding permission, write to Bellwether Media, Inc., Attention: Permissions Department, 3500 American Blvd W, Suite 150, Bloomington, MN 55431

Library of Congress Cataloging-in-Publication Data

Names: Ross, Melissa, author.
Title: Famous athletes / By Melissa Ross.
Description: Eureka! | Minnetonka, MN : Bellwether Media, Inc., 2026. | Series: Legends and game changers | Includes index. | Audience: Ages 9-15 | Audience: Grades 7-9 | Summary: "Engaging images accompany information on famous athletes. The text level and subject matter are intended for students in grades 5 through 9"-- Provided by publisher.
Identifiers: LCCN 2025020015 (print) | LCCN 2025020016 (ebook) | ISBN 9798893045536 (library binding) | ISBN 9798893046915 (ebook)
Subjects: LCSH: Athletes--Biography--Juvenile literature.
Classification: LCC GV697.A1 R68 2026 (print) | LCC GV697.A1 (ebook) | DDC 796.092/2--dc23/eng/20250520
LC record available at https://lccn.loc.gov/2025020015
LC ebook record available at https://lccn.loc.gov/2025020016

Text copyright © 2026 by Bellwether Media, Inc. EUREKA! and associated logos are trademarks and/or registered trademarks of Bellwether Media, Inc. Bellwether Media is a division of FlutterBee Education Group.

Editor: Betsy Rathburn Series Designer: Jeffrey Kollock Book Designer: Josh Brink

Printed in the United States of America, North Mankato, MN.

TABLE OF CONTENTS

SPORTS HISTORY 4

FOOTBALL PLAYERS 8

SOCCER PLAYERS 12

BASEBALL PLAYERS 16

BASKETBALL PLAYERS 20

HOCKEY PLAYERS 26

TENNIS PLAYERS 30

OLYMPIANS AND PARALYMPIANS 34

THE FUTURE OF SPORTS 44

GLOSSARY 46

WRITE ABOUT IT! 47

INDEX 48

SPORTS HISTORY

Sports help people stay healthy. They help people get exercise, supporting their physical and mental well-being. Sports also bring people together. People meet others they might not normally spend time with. This builds bonds and strengthens communities.

Sports have played a role throughout history. The first modern Olympic Games were held in 1896 in Athens, Greece. At that time, only **amateur** male athletes competed. Women first competed in the Olympics in 1900. Today, **professional** athletes are allowed. There are hundreds of events!

Sports have been popular outside of the Olympics, too. Many popular sports were invented in the 1700s and 1800s. Other sports grew over time. As new machines were invented in the 1800s, people spent less time working. More people had free time to play sports.

Eventually, official rules were created for each sport. Small clubs gave way to large, organized leagues. New leagues are still created today. In 2023, the Professional Women's Hockey League (PWHL) began its first season.

TIMELINE

1877 the first Wimbledon tennis championship is held

1891 basketball is created by James Naismith

1896
the first modern Olympic Games are held

1903
the first World Series is played

1904
FIFA is formed

1917
the NHL is formed

1920
the NFL forms as the American Professional Football Association

1949
the NBA is formed

1997
the first WNBA game is played

2023
the first season of the PWHL begins

FOOTBALL

The National Football League (NFL) was formed in 1920. Today, 32 teams play in the league.

BASEBALL

In 1903, the first World Series in Major League Baseball (MLB) was played. The top team from the American League (AL) and the National League (NL) faced each other.

BASKETBALL

James Naismith invented basketball in 1891. In 1949, the National Basketball Association (NBA) formed. The Women's National Basketball Association (WNBA) started in 1997.

MORE SPORTS, MORE ATHLETES!

SOCCER

The Fédération Internationale de Football Association (FIFA) formed in Switzerland in 1904. In the United States, Major League Soccer (MLS) began playing in 1996.

ICE HOCKEY

The National Hockey League (NHL) formed in Canada in 1917. In 2023, the PWHL formed.

TENNIS

The first Wimbledon was held in 1877. It became one of four **Grand Slam** tournaments. The others are the Australian Open, the French Open, and the U.S. Open.

THE OLYMPIC GAMES

The first Olympic Games were held in Greece in 776 BCE. The modern Olympics began in 1896 CE.

TONY HAWK

Tony Hawk is a skateboarding champion. Nicknamed Birdman, he is the first person to land a 900 in competition. This trick involves spinning in the air two-and-a-half times. He has won 16 medals in the X Games.

BETHANY HAMILTON

When she was 13 years old, Bethany Hamilton survived a shark attack while surfing. She lost her arm. But she did not give up her favorite sport. Today, she is a professional surfer with several championships under her belt.

CHLOE KIM

At age 14, Chloe Kim won the snowboarding superpipe event at the X Games. At the time, she was the event's youngest ever winner. Three years later, she became the youngest woman to win an Olympic gold medal in the snowboarding half-pipe event!

NELLY KORDA

Nelly Korda is a professional golfer with many championships. She has won the Ladies Professional Golf Association tour 15 times. She is also an Olympic gold medalist. Her skill on the golf course has sent her to the top of the women's golf rankings.

FOOTBALL PLAYERS

Many consider Tom Brady to be the greatest football player of all time. His combined 23 seasons with the New England Patriots and the Tampa Bay Buccaneers will go down in NFL history!

Tom Brady

THE BRADY BUNCH

Growing up, Brady often attended San Francisco 49ers games with his family. In high school, he played baseball and football. He was selected in the 1995 MLB **draft**, but he decided to play football for the University of Michigan instead. After graduating, he was drafted by the New England Patriots in 2000. He became their backup **quarterback**.

ON TO THE SUPER BOWL

In 2001, the Patriots' starting quarterback was injured. Brady stepped in. That season, he led the Patriots to their first Super Bowl championship. Six more followed, with the sixth win in 2019. In 2020, Brady started playing for the Tampa Bay Buccaneers. He won his seventh Super Bowl in his second season with the team. In 2023, Brady retired from football.

A NEW CHAPTER

Brady retired from playing, but he is not done with football. In 2024, he started working as an **analyst** during NFL games.

HALL OF FAMER

Brady has more Super Bowl wins than any other player. His performance earned him a spot in the New England Patriots Hall of Fame in 2024.

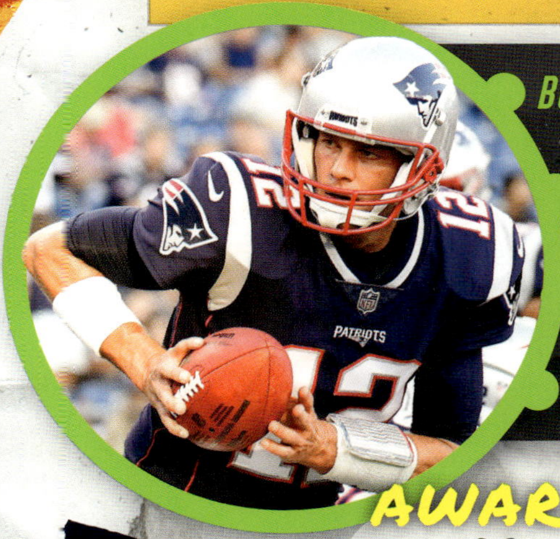

BORN: August 3, 1977, in San Mateo, California

EDUCATION: University of Michigan

TEAMS: New England Patriots, Tampa Bay Buccaneers

POSITION: quarterback

AWARDS AND HONORS

- 3 NFL MVP awards
- 7 Super Bowl championships
- 5 Super Bowl MVP awards
- 1 Associated Press NFL Comeback Player of the Year Award
- 2 Offensive Player of the Year awards

SUPER BOWL STAR

Brady has appeared in 10 Super Bowls, the most of any quarterback in history.

TIMELINE

2000 is chosen by the New England Patriots in the sixth round of the NFL draft

2001 takes over as starting quarterback

2002 leads the Patriots to a Super Bowl win and receives his first Super Bowl MVP award

2019 leads the Patriots to their sixth Super Bowl win

2021 leads the Tampa Bay Buccaneers to the seventh Super Bowl win of his career

Patrick Mahomes

Patrick Mahomes is a top quarterback who has led the Kansas City Chiefs to three Super Bowl wins. He has set many NFL records in his young career.

CHOOSING FOOTBALL

Mahomes grew up in Tyler, Texas. He excelled at baseball, basketball, and football in high school. In 2014, he was picked by the Detroit Tigers in the MLB draft. He chose to play football for Texas Tech University instead.

QUARTERBACK STAR

In 2016, Mahomes earned the Sammy Baugh Trophy for being the best college football passer. The next year, he was drafted by the Kansas City Chiefs. As quarterback, he led the team to a Super Bowl win in 2020. The next year, the Chiefs made it to the Super Bowl again. But they lost. Mahomes did not give up. He led the Chiefs to win the Super Bowl in 2023 and 2024!

A BUSINESSMAN, TOO!

In 2019, Mahomes started 15 and the Mahomies. This foundation helps children in need. In 2020, he became part-owner of the Kansas City Royals baseball team. He also owns two soccer teams and a pickleball club.

TIMELINE

2017 is selected 10th overall by the Kansas City Chiefs in the NFL draft

2019 establishes 15 and the Mahomies foundation

2020 wins his first Super Bowl

RECORD SETTER

Mahomes still has a long career ahead. He has already set several NFL records, including being the fastest player to 25,000 career passing yards in NFL history. He did it in 83 games!

AWARDS AND HONORS

- 2 NFL MVP awards
- 3 Super Bowl championships
- 3 Super Bowl MVP awards
- 1 Associated Press Offensive Player of the Year award
- 1 ESPY Award for Best NFL Player

BORN: September 17, 1995, in Tyler, Texas

EDUCATION: Texas Tech University

TEAM: Kansas City Chiefs

POSITION: quarterback

2023 sets the record for combined passing and rushing yards in a season with 5,614 yards

2024 wins his third Super Bowl and third Super Bowl MVP award

2025 plays in his fifth Super Bowl

SOCCER PLAYERS

During her career, Alex Morgan was known as a talented soccer **forward**. She had excellent speed and scoring ability.

ALL-AMERICAN

Alex Morgan grew up in California. She began playing club soccer at age 14. In high school, the National Soccer Coaches of America named her All-American. In 2007, she began playing soccer at the University of California, Berkeley.

Alex Morgan

SAN DIMAS

BORN: July 2, 1989, in San Dimas, California

EDUCATION: University of California, Berkeley

TEAMS: U.S. Women's National Soccer Team, San Diego Wave FC, Orlando Pride, Portland Thorns, Seattle Sounders Women, Western New York Flash

POSITION: forward

GOING PRO

After college, Morgan played for the Western New York Flash. She soon moved to play for the Portland Thorns. She won the National Women's Soccer League (NWSL) championship with them in 2013. In 2021, she joined the San Diego Wave. The next year, her team finished the season with the best record, winning the NWSL Shield.

INTERNATIONAL SOCCER

Morgan won her first World Cup in 2015. She won it again four years later, earning the Silver Boot for the second-most goals scored during the tournament. She is also an Olympian with a gold and a bronze medal.

OTHER TALENTS

Morgan is the author of a series of fiction books about soccer. In 2018, she starred in a soccer movie called *Alex and Me*.

FIGHTING FOR FAIRNESS

In 2019, Alex and other U.S. Women's National Soccer Team players **sued** the U.S. Soccer Federation for gender **discrimination**. The federation was forced to pay all players equally.

AWARDS AND HONORS

- 1 Olympic gold medal
- 3-time FIFA World Player of the Year finalist
- 2 World Cup championships
- 1 Olympic bronze medal
- 1 ESPY Award for Best Female Athlete

TIMELINE

- **2011** begins playing soccer professionally
- **2012** wins an Olympic gold medal
- **2015** wins her first World Cup
- **2019** wins her second World cup
- **2024** retires from professional soccer

Lionel Messi

Lionel Messi is a top soccer player known for his ability to score on the field. His World Cup wins and success with FC Barcelona make him one of soccer's greatest players.

TIMELINE

- **2004** begins playing for Barcelona
- **2008** wins an Olympic Gold medal
- **2010** wins the first of eight Trofeo Pichichi Awards
- **2022** leads Argentina to win the FIFA World Cup
- **2023** wins his 8th Ballon d'Or award

GROWING PROBLEMS

Messi was born in Argentina. He began playing soccer with his brothers when he was young. When he was 10, he was diagnosed with a disease that slows growth. His family moved to Spain after a soccer academy offered to pay for treatments. At age 17, Messi scored his first goal for FC Barcelona.

RECORD SETTER

Messi played for Barcelona for 17 seasons. In 2007, he made his first of 36 **hat tricks** for Barcelona. In 2012, he broke a season record by scoring 91 goals! During his time with Barcleona, Messi won 35 trophies and set a club record of 672 goals scored.

BORN: June 24, 1987, in Rosario, Argentina

TEAMS: FC Barcelona, Paris Saint-Germain FC, Inter Miami CF, Argentine national team

POSITION: forward

THE WORLD STAGE

Messi played for Argentina's national team, too. He led Argentina in five World Cups between 2006 and 2022. They finally won in 2022! In 2024, Messi led Argentina to win the Copa América tournament.

HELPING CHILDREN

In 2007, Messi began the Leo Messi Foundation, which helps support children in need. In 2010, he became **Ambassador** to UNICEF, an organization that helps children in poverty.

MOST DECORATED

Messi is the most decorated soccer player in the world with 45 trophies. In 2024, he became the second-highest soccer scorer of all time!

AWARDS AND HONORS

- 1 Olympic gold medal
- 1 FIFA World Cup win
- 8 Trofeo Pichichi awards
- 8 Ballon d'Or awards
- 2 Copa América wins
- 9 La Liga Player of the Year awards

"You have to fight to reach your dream. You have to sacrifice and work hard for it."
— Lionel Messi

OTHER TEAMS

Messi left Barcelona in 2021 to play for Paris Saint-Germain. In 2023, he began playing for Inter Miami.

BASEBALL PLAYERS

During his professional career, Mike Trout has stood out as a talented center fielder and a powerful hitter. He has broken records, won awards, and earned a place as one of baseball's most talented players.

Mike Trout

BEGINNING TO BREAK RECORDS

Trout grew up in New Jersey. His dad introduced him to baseball. During Trout's high school career, he pitched a no-hitter game with 18 strikeouts. It broke a New Jersey high school record!

OFF TO THE PROS

In 2009, Trout was drafted by the Los Angeles Angels. He played his first game with them in 2011. He played as a center fielder. He also showed off his batting skills. In 2012, Trout became the first player to hit 30 home runs, steal 45 bases, and score 125 runs in a single season. He also won the AL **Rookie** of the Year award. He continues to play well and set records. In 2023, he hit his 300th double!

HELPING OTHERS

Trout works with the Make-A-Wish Foundation, which grants the wishes of children with serious illnesses. He was also named Mental Wellness Ambassador for Major League Baseball in 2023.

ONE OF THE GREATS

Trout is considered one of the greatest all-around professional baseball players in the world. He is an 11-time All-Star. He won the AL MVP award three times and the All-Star MVP award twice.

BORN: August 7, 1991, in Vineland, New Jersey

EDUCATION: Millville Senior High School

TEAM: Los Angeles Angels

POSITION: center fielder

AWARDS AND HONORS

- 1 AL Rookie of the Year award
- 3 AL MVP awards
- 2 MLB All-Star MVP awards
- 2 Hank Aaron Awards
- 9 Silver Slugger Awards

THE CLASSIC SILVER WIN

Trout led his team to a silver medal win in 2023 at the World Baseball Classic.

TIMELINE

2009 drafted by the Los Angeles Angels

2012 becomes the youngest player to win the AL Rookie of the Year award

2019 wins his third AL MVP award

2020 hits his 300th career home run

2023 hits the 300th double of his career

Shohei Ohtani

Shohei Ohtani is a baseball superstar. His fast pitching and powerful hitting make him a threat on the mound and at the plate. He has won awards, set records, and represented his native Japan in the World Baseball Classic!

LIGHTNING SPEED

Ohtani was born in Japan. He began playing baseball at age 8 and became one of Japan's top players in high school. His pitching speed was 99 miles (159 kilometers) per hour! In 2012, he started playing for the Hokkaido Nippon Ham Fighters in Japan.

MOVING TO THE MLB

In 2017, Ohtani moved to the U.S. to play for the Los Angeles Angels. The following year, he was named the AL's Rookie of the Year. In 2021, he hit 46 home runs and stole 26 bases. As a pitcher, he struck out 156 batters. In 2023, he switched teams to the Los Angeles Dodgers. The following year, he helped the Dodgers win the World Series!

AMONG THE GREATS

Ohtani is one of few people in history to hit at least 10 home runs and earn 10 wins as a pitcher in the same season.

TIMELINE

2016
leads the Hokkaido Nippon Ham Fighters to Pacific League and Japan Series championships

2017
signs with the Los Angeles Angels

GIVING BIG

In 2023, Ohtani donated around 60,000 baseball gloves to elementary schools in Japan. The following year, he and the Dodgers gave $1 million to people affected by an earthquake in Japan.

TOP PICK!

Ohtani is the first baseball player to win a **unanimous** vote twice for the AL MVP award.

AWARDS AND HONORS

- 4 Edgar Martínez Awards
- 1 World Series championship
- 3 Silver Slugger Awards
- 2 Hank Aaron Awards
- 2 AL MVP awards
- 1 AL Rookie of the Year award

BORN: July 5, 1994, in Oshu, Japan

TEAMS: Hokkaido Nippon Ham Fighters, Los Angeles Angels, Los Angeles Dodgers

POSITIONS: pitcher, designated hitter

2018 wins AL Rookie of the Year award

2021 wins his first AL MVP award

2024 wins the World Series with the Los Angeles Dodgers

BASKETBALL PLAYERS

Over more than 20 seasons, LeBron James has stood out as one of the NBA's most talented players. His elite shooting skills, passing ability, and teamwork make him a basketball star!

EARLY TALENT

Early in life, James showed talent in basketball. He was **recruited** to play for a private high school in Akron, Ohio. He helped his team win three Division III state titles.

NEW TEAMS

After high school, James was drafted by the Cleveland Cavaliers. The team made it to the NBA Finals in 2007 but lost. In 2010, James started playing for the Miami Heat, leading them to win NBA championships in 2012 and 2013.

A CHAMPIONSHIP AT LAST

In 2014, James went back to the Cavaliers. He led them to their first NBA championship in 2016. In 2018, James joined the Los Angeles Lakers, where he won his fourth championship in 2020. In 2023, he played in the first-ever NBA Cup and was named its MVP!

NICE SHOES!

James has a lifetime partnership with Nike. In 2003, he launched his own line of Nike shoes. More than 20 different styles have been released.

ALWAYS ON TOP

James is one of basketball's most accomplished players. When he retires, he will likely be added to the Naismith Memorial Basketball Hall of Fame!

AWARDS AND HONORS

- 1 NBA Rookie of the Year award
- 3 Olympic gold medals
- 1 Olympic bronze medal
- 4 NBA championships
- 4 NBA MVP awards
- 4 NBA Finals MVP awards
- 1 NBA Cup

BORN: December 30, 1984, in Akron, Ohio

TEAMS: Cleveland Cavaliers, Miami Heat, Los Angeles Lakers, U.S. national team

POSITIONS: small forward, shooting guard

MOVIE STAR

In 2021, James starred in a movie called *Space Jam: A New Legacy*.

TIMELINE

2003 is drafted to the Cavaliers as the first all-around NBA pick

2013 wins his second NBA Championship with the Miami Heat

2016 leads the Cavaliers to their first championship

2018 joins the Los Angeles Lakers

2024 wins his third Olympic gold medal

Diana Taurasi

Diana Taurasi is the top scorer in U.S. women's basketball history. She dominated the court, making plays, scoring points, and leading her team to big wins.

TIMELINE

2000 wins the Naismith Award for the national girls' high school basketball player of the year

2003 wins second national college championship

2004 is selected by the Phoenix Mercury in the WNBA draft

2014 wins third WNBA championship

2024 wins 6th Olympic gold medal

A YOUNG ATHLETE

Taurasi grew up in Chino, California. She enjoyed playing basketball and soccer from a young age. In high school, she chose to focus on basketball. In 2000, she earned the Naismith Award for national girls' high school basketball player of the year.

FROM COLLEGE TO PRO

Taurasi attended the University of Connecticut after high school. She led the women's basketball team to three championship wins. In 2004, Taurasi joined the Phoenix Mercury. Two years later, she was the WNBA's scoring leader for the first time. She earned this title again every year from 2008 to 2011. With her scoring skills, the Mercury earned championship wins in 2007, 2009, and 2014.

THE GOAL OF GIVING

In 2006, Taurasi partnered with KaBOOM. This organization provides safe playgrounds for kids across the U.S. In 2018, she received the WNBA Community Assist Award for her work supporting single mothers and the **LGBTQ+** community.

GOLD MEDALIST

Outside of the WNBA, Taurasi is an Olympian. She earned a gold with Team USA at every Olympic Games between 2004 and 2024.

POINTS LEADER

Taurasi retired from basketball in 2025. She is the top scorer in WNBA history with 10,646 points.

BORN: June 11, 1982, in Glendale, California

EDUCATION: University of Connecticut

TEAMS: Phoenix Mercury, U.S. national team

POSITION: guard

AWARDS AND HONORS

- 1 WNBA Rookie of the Year award
- 3 WNBA championships
- 6 Olympic gold medals
- 2 WNBA Finals MVP awards

Michael Jordan

Michael Jordan is considered one of the best basketball players ever. Nicknamed "His Airness" thanks to his ability to slam dunk, he has six NBA championship wins.

A LOVE FOR COMPETITION

Jordan grew up in Wilmington, North Carolina. From a young age, he liked to compete. During his second year in high school, Jordan was disappointed that he did not make the **varsity** team. But he worked hard and made it the following year. In 1981, he was recruited to play for the University of North Carolina at Chapel Hill. In his first year, he made the winning basket at the national championship game.

A CHAMPION LEADER

Jordan left college early to play for the Chicago Bulls. In 1990, he scored a career-high 69 points in one game. The following year, he led the Bulls to their first NBA championship. Five more followed throughout the 1990s. In 1999, Jordan announced his retirement. But in 2001, he came out of retirement to play two seasons with the Washington Wizards.

A SHOE DESIGNER

Jordan partnered with Nike in 1984 to produce his own line of sneakers. A new Air Jordan design was released every season Jordan played!

TIMELINE

1984 joins the Chicago Bulls

1988 is selected as NBA MVP for the first time

1992 wins his second Olympic gold medal

ONE OF THE GREATS

Jordan was the NBA's top scorer 10 times during his career, the most in NBA history. In 2009, he was added to the Naismith Memorial Basketball Hall of Fame.

BORN: February 17, 1963, in Brooklyn, New York

EDUCATION: University of North Carolina at Chapel Hill

TEAMS: Chicago Bulls, Washington Wizards, U.S. national team

POSITIONS: shooting guard, small forward

AWARDS AND HONORS

- 6 NBA championships
- 6 NBA Finals MVP awards
- 2 Olympic gold medals
- 1 Defensive Player of the Year award
- 2 NBA Slam Dunk Contest wins
- 1 Rookie of the Year award

THE DREAM TEAM

Jordan played in the 1992 Olympic Games with what became known as the "Dream Team." It was made up of other famous players, including Charles Barkley, Magic Johnson, and Larry Bird.

1998 wins his 6th NBA championship

2003 plays his last game in the NBA with the Washington Wizards and retires

2009 is inducted into the Naismith Memorial Basketball Hall of Fame

HOCKEY PLAYERS

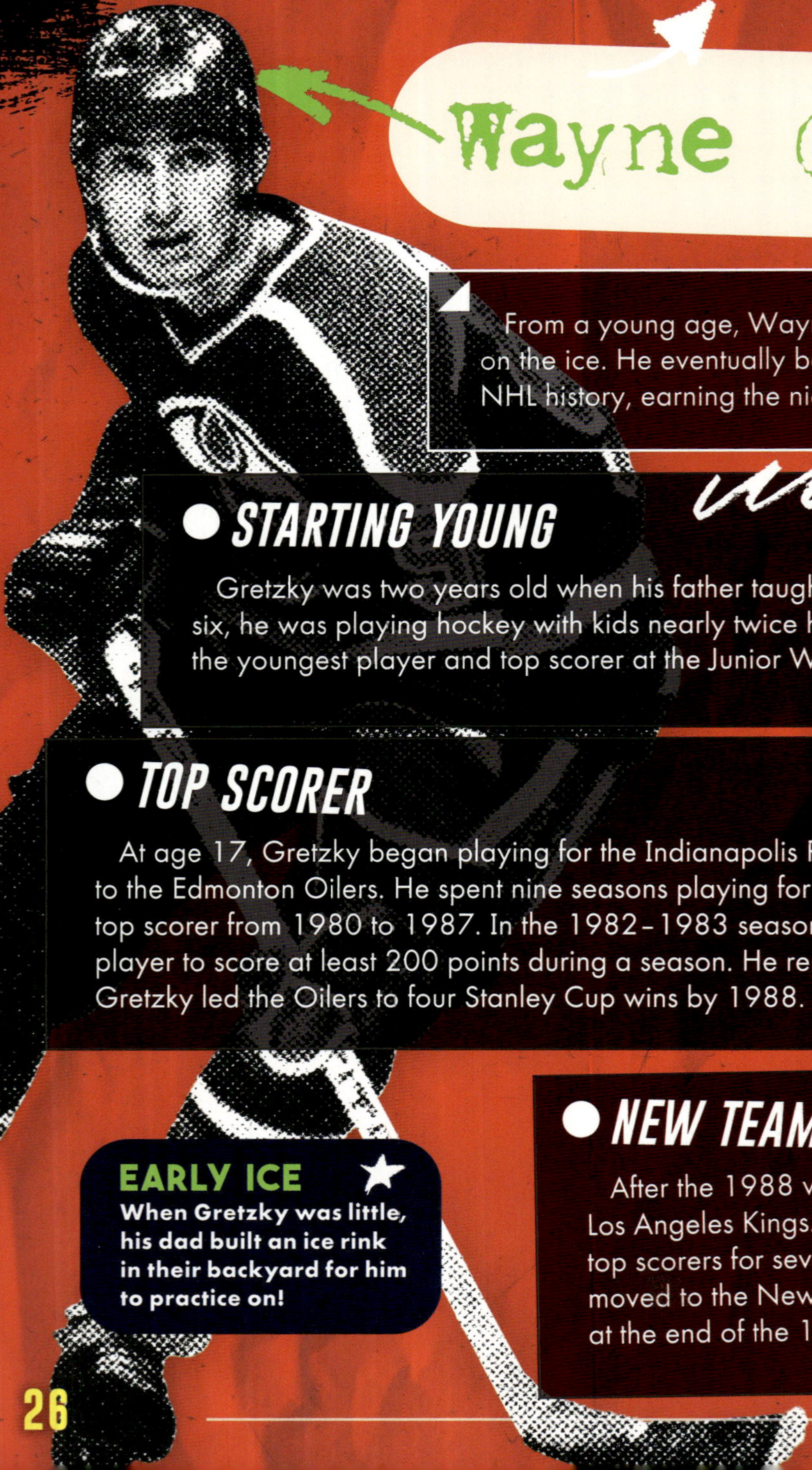

Wayne Gretzky

From a young age, Wayne Gretzky showed talent on the ice. He eventually became the top scorer in NHL history, earning the nickname "The Great One."

STARTING YOUNG

Gretzky was two years old when his father taught him to skate. By age six, he was playing hockey with kids nearly twice his age. In 1978, he was the youngest player and top scorer at the Junior World Championships.

TOP SCORER

At age 17, Gretzky began playing for the Indianapolis Racers. He soon moved to the Edmonton Oilers. He spent nine seasons playing for them. He was the NHL's top scorer from 1980 to 1987. In the 1982–1983 season, he became the first-ever player to score at least 200 points during a season. He repeated this three more times. Gretzky led the Oilers to four Stanley Cup wins by 1988.

NEW TEAMS

After the 1988 win, Gretzky moved to the Los Angeles Kings. He was among the NHL's top scorers for several years. In 1996, he moved to the New York Rangers. He retired at the end of the 1999 season.

EARLY ICE
When Gretzky was little, his dad built an ice rink in their backyard for him to practice on!

HOCKEY CONTINUES

Gretzky established the Wayne Gretzky Foundation in 2002. The organization helps kids learn hockey. In 2021, Gretzky became an NHL sports analyst.

RECORD HOLDER

Gretzky is the top scorer and has the most **assists** in NHL history. In 1999, he was **inducted** into the Hockey Hall of Fame.

BORN: January 26, 1961, in Brantford, Ontario, Canada

TEAMS: Indianapolis Racers, Edmonton Oilers, Los Angeles Kings, St. Louis Blues, New York Rangers, Canadian national team

POSITION: center

AWARDS AND HONORS

- 2 Conn Smythe Trophies
- 4 Stanley Cup championships
- 9 Hart Memorial Trophies
- 5 Ted Lindsay Awards
- 10 Art Ross Trophies
- 1 Lou Kaplan Rookie of the Year award

TIMELINE

1978 plays in the World Junior Championships and leads the tournament in scoring

1979 joins the Edmonton Oilers

1982–1983 becomes the first player to score 200 points in a season

1988 wins his fourth Stanley Cup with the Edmonton Oilers

1999 retires and is inducted into the Hockey Hall of Fame

Connor McDavid

Connor McDavid is a Canadian hockey player. At 19 years old, he became the NHL's youngest-ever team captain. Since then, his career has only gotten brighter.

A YOUNG PLAYER

McDavid grew up in Canada, playing hockey from a young age. He began playing for the Ontario Hockey League's Erie Otters in 2012 when he was 15.

GOING PRO

McDavid joined the Edmonton Oilers in 2015. In the 2016–2017 season, he helped the Oilers reach the Stanley Cup **playoffs** for the first time since 2006. They lost, but it gave many hope that they could make it again. McDavid achieved his highest points-scoring season in the 2022–2023 season with 153 points.

MORE STANLEY CHANCES

McDavid led the Oilers to the Stanley Cup finals in 2024. After losing the first three games, McDavid scored four points each to win the next two. The Oilers lost in Game 7. McDavid led the Oilers back to the Stanley Cup finals in 2025.

"The beauty of hockey players is that they make everyone feel included and make everyone feel a part of it."
— Connor McDavid

HELPING KIDS

In 2017, McDavid worked with Hockey Helps Kids. This organization helps teach kids leadership and athletic skills. He has also worked with the Ben Stelter Foundation. It raises money to help families of kids with cancer.

LEAVING A LEGACY

In his young career, McDavid has already risen to the top in the NHL. He is the fourth player in NHL history to record 100 assists in one season.

BORN: January 13, 1997, in Richmond Hill, Ontario, Canada

TEAM: Edmonton Oilers

POSITION: center

AWARDS AND HONORS

- 3 Hart Memorial Trophies
- 4 Ted Lindsay Awards
- 5 Art Ross Trophies
- 1 Maurice "Rocket" Richard Trophy

TIMELINE

- **2012** starts playing for the Erie Otters
- **2015** starts playing for the Edmonton Oilers
- **2017** becomes the leading scorer in the NHL
- **2018** wins second Ted Lindsay Award as the most outstanding NHL player
- **2022–2023** achieves his highest point-scoring season with 153 points
- **2025** leads the Oilers to the Stanley Cup finals

TENNIS PLAYERS

Rafael Nadal is among the world's the top tennis players. Known for his dominance on clay courts, he is often called the "King of Clay." His record of 14 French Open wins will likely stand for many years!

Rafael Nadal

LEFTY LEARNING

Nadal grew up on the island of Mallorca, Spain. When Nadal was young, his uncle began teaching him tennis. He encouraged Nadal to play left-handed. This gave Nadal an advantage against right-handed players.

FRENCH OPEN

In 2005, Nadal won his first Grand Slam title at the French Open. He continued to excel at this competition. By 2022, he had earned 14 French Open titles.

CAREER GRAND SLAM

After his first French Open win, Nadal won his first of two Wimbledon titles in 2008. The following year, he won his first of two Australian Open titles. He only needed to win the U.S. Open to earn his career Grand Slam. He did it in 2010!

GOLDEN SLAM

Nadal has also achieved a Golden Slam. This is when players earn an Olympic gold medal along with a career Grand Slam.

ON THE DOUBLE

Nadal also played doubles tennis. He has 15 doubles titles, including a gold medal from the 2016 Olympic Games.

TRAINING OTHERS

In 2010, Nadal created the Rafa Nadal Foundation, which provides education and sports programs for children. In 2016, Nadal established the Rafa Nadal Academy. It offers tennis training programs.

RECORD HOLDER

Nadal won 22 Grand Slam men's singles titles, including a record 14 French Open titles.

BORN: June 3, 1986, in Manacor, Mallorca, Spain

TEAM: Spanish national team

COMPETITIONS: singles and doubles

MANACOR, MALLORCA

TIMELINE

- **2005** wins his first French Open
- **2008** wins his first Wimbledon title
- **2009** wins his first Australian Open title
- **2010** completes his career Grand Slam with a U.S. Open win
- **2022** sets a new record of 14 French Open wins
- **2024** retires from professional tennis

AWARDS AND HONORS

- 14 French Open titles
- 4 U.S. Open titles
- 2 Wimbledon titles
- 2 Australian Open titles
- 2 Olympic gold medals
- Grand Cross of the Royal Order of Sporting Merit

Serena Williams

Serena Williams is a tennis powerhouse considered one of the best players of all time. During her career, she earned top titles in both doubles and singles tennis.

EARLY RANKING

Williams grew up in California. She and her sister Venus learned to play tennis from their dad. Early on, Serena ranked high in juniors tennis. She turned professional in 1995 at the age of 14. She won the 1999 U.S. Open women's singles tournament at 17.

DOUBLE TROUBLE

Williams also played doubles tennis with Venus. Together, they earned 14 Grand Slam titles and 3 Olympic medals.

SLAMMING THE RECORDS

In 2000, Williams won her first Olympic gold medal in doubles with Venus. She won her first singles French Open and Wimbledon titles in 2002. In 2003, she won her first Australian Open, completing her career Grand Slam. Between February 2013 and September 2016, she was the top-ranked women's player for 186 weeks in a row. She retired in 2022.

BEYOND TENNIS

In 2017, Williams helped establish the Yetunde Price Resource Center. The center offers programs to help people affected by violence. Williams also wrote an **autobiography** published in 2009.

ON HER OWN

Williams is the only player to accomplish a career Grand Slam in both singles and doubles tennis.

TIMELINE

1999 wins her first Grand Slam singles title

2000 wins her first Olympic gold medal in doubles with sister Venus

BORN: September 26, 1981, in Saginaw, Michigan

TEAM: U.S. national team

COMPETITIONS: singles and doubles

TITLE HOLDER

Williams won 39 major tennis titles, including 23 Grand Slam singles wins. She was inducted into the National Women's Hall of Fame in 2024.

AWARDS AND HONORS

- 23 singles Grand Slam titles
- 14 doubles Grand Slam titles
- 3 Olympic gold medals in doubles
- 1 Olympic gold medal in singles

2012 wins two Olympic gold medals, one in singles and one in doubles

2016 wins her 14th Grand Slam in doubles

2017 wins her 23rd Grand Slam in singles

OLYMPIANS AND PARALYMPIANS

Known for his powerful butterfly stroke, Michael Phelps is one of the world's top swimmers. He set many world records and is the most decorated Olympian of all time.

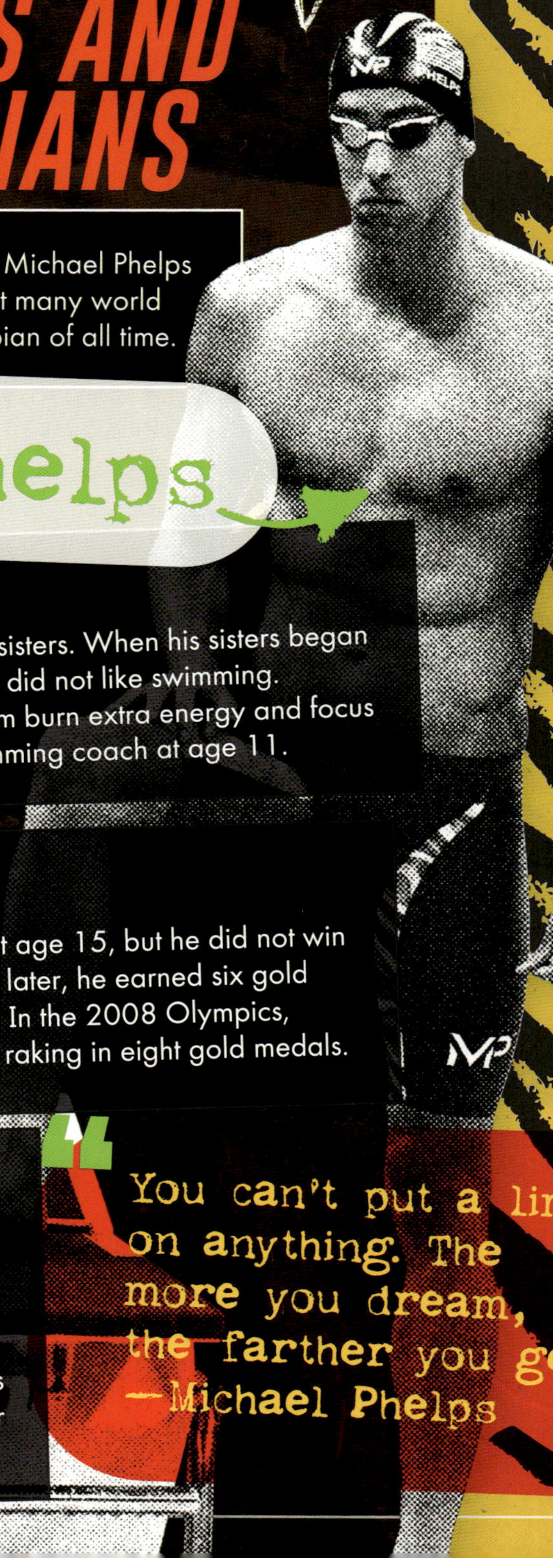

Michael Phelps

BURNING ENERGY

Phelps grew up with his mom and two sisters. When his sisters began swimming, he followed along. At first, he did not like swimming. But eventually, he found that it helped him burn extra energy and focus in school. He began training with a swimming coach at age 11.

THE ROAD TO GOLD

Phelps competed in his first Olympics at age 15, but he did not win any medals. He kept training. Four years later, he earned six gold and two bronze medals at the Olympics. In the 2008 Olympics, Phelps won every event he competed in, raking in eight gold medals.

RECORD SETTER

In 2003, Phelps set a record in the 100-meter butterfly. It was soon broken, but Phelps set a new record in 2009 with a time of 49.82 seconds. It stood for 10 years. At the 2008 Olympics, his team set the record for the 4x100-meter **relay**. It still stands today!

"You can't put a limit on anything. The more you dream, the farther you get."
—Michael Phelps

HELPING OTHERS

In 2008, Phelps began the Michael Phelps Foundation. It promotes water safety and healthy living.

SWIMMING FORWARD

Phelps retired in 2016. But his legacy lives on. In 2023, he was added to the International Swimming Hall of Fame.

BORN: June 30, 1985, in Baltimore, Maryland

TEAM: U.S. national team

EVENTS: butterfly, individual medley, individual freestyle, medley relay, freestyle relay

AWARDS AND HONORS

- 23 Olympic gold medals
- 3 Olympic silver medals
- 2 Olympic Bronze medals
- 33 World Athletics Championships medals
- 32 Swimming World Cup medals

TIMELINE

- **2004** wins 6 gold medals and 2 bronze medals at the Athens Olympics
- **2008** becomes the first athlete to win 8 gold medals in a single Olympic Games
- **2012** wins 4 gold medals and 2 silver medals at the London Olympics
- **2016** wins 5 gold medals and 1 silver medal at the Rio de Janeiro Olympics
- **2023** is inducted into the International Swimming Hall of Fame

Michelle Kwan

Michelle Kwan is the most decorated figure skater in U.S. history. Known for her difficult routines and complicated moves, she earned 43 championship titles.

YOUNG WINNER

Kwan's parents moved from Hong Kong to California before she was born. At age 5, Kwan started ice skating lessons. She became a senior-level skater by age 12. In 1994, she won the silver medal at the U.S. Nationals.

WINNING THE WORLD

In 1996, Kwan won both the World Championship and the U.S. Nationals for the first time. She became known for her graceful skating and complex moves. In 1998, she was the first female skater to earn a perfect score in the U.S. Nationals short program. She won the national title for the next 8 consecutive years.

AWARDS AND HONORS

- 1 Olympic silver medal
- 9 U.S. Nationals titles
- 5 World Championship titles
- 1 Olympic bronze medal

OLYMPIAN

Kwan first competed in the Olympics in 1998. She earned a silver medal. She returned to the Olympics in 2002, hoping for a gold. She earned a bronze. She never won gold, but she is considered one of the best ice skaters in U.S. history!

TIMELINE

1994 wins silver at the U.S. Figure Skating Championships

1996 wins both the U.S. Nationals and the World Figure Skating Championships

1998 earns a perfect score at the U.S. Nationals

BORN: July 7, 1980, in Torrance, California

EDUCATION: University of Denver, Tufts University

EVENT: singles figure skating

TEAM: U.S. national team

HELPING OTHERS WIN

Kwan retired from skating in 2006. In 2011, she earned a master's degree in international relations. She served as U.S. Ambassador to Belize from 2022 to 2025.

ONE OF THE BEST

In 2012, Kwan was inducted into the Figure Skating Hall of Fame. In 2022, she was inducted into the U.S. Olympic & Paralympic Hall of Fame.

2003 wins her fifth world championship

2005 wins her ninth U.S. championship

2022 is appointed U.S. Ambassador to Belize

Usain Bolt

Jamaican sprinter Usain Bolt is often called the fastest man in the world. Known as "Lightning Bolt," his records in the 100-meter and 200-meter races have stood for more than a decade.

A BORN RUNNER

Bolt grew up enjoying cricket and soccer. His coaches noticed his natural running speed and encouraged him to try track and field. At age 15, he won the gold medal in the 200-meter at the 2002 Junior World Championships.

BREAKING RECORDS

Five years later, Bolt won a silver medal in the 200-meter at the 2007 World Championships. His second-place finish prompted him to work harder. In 2008, he ran the 100-meter in 9.72 seconds, breaking the world record. He broke it again the next year, running it in 9.58 seconds.

AWARDS AND HONORS

- 8 Olympic gold medals
- 11 World Championships gold medals
- 2 World Championships silver medals
- 3 ESPY Awards for Best International Athlete
- 1 World Championships bronze medal

BECOMING AN OLYMPIAN

In 2008, Bolt won Olympic gold medals in the 100-meter, 200-meter, and 4x100-meter relay events. His relay medal was later stripped because of his teammate's misconduct. He returned to the Olympics in 2012, winning three more golds in the same events. He did it again in 2016! In total, he has eight Olympic gold medals.

BUILDING A FOUNDATION

Bolt started the Usain Bolt Foundation in 2010. The organization provides education and helps children in Jamaica.

BORN: August 21, 1986, in Sherwood Content, Jamaica

TEAM: Jamaican national team

EVENTS: 100-meter, 200-meter, 4x100-meter relay

STILL A RECORD HOLDER

Bolt set records in the 100-meter and 200-meter races. His times of 9.58 seconds and 19.19 seconds still stand today!

TIMELINE

2002 wins a gold medal at the Junior World Championships

2007 wins silver for the 200-meter in the World Championships

2008 wins his first Olympic gold medals

2009 sets world record times in the 100-meter and 200-meter

2012 wins 3 Olympic gold medals

2016 wins 3 more Olympic gold medals

Simone Biles

Simone Biles is the most decorated gymnast in history. She has earned more than 100 medals, including 11 Olympic medals. She has even created signature moves that are named after her!

STARING EARLY

When she was six, Biles visited a gymnastics center in Houston, Texas. Soon after, she began training there. At age 11, she competed in her first junior national competition. She placed third all-around and first in **vault**.

WORLD CHAMPION

At the 2018 World Championships, Biles won three gold medals, one silver medal, and one bronze medal. The next year, she won five gold medals. She also showed off two new moves, which included flips, twists, and a special **dismount**. These moves were named after her!

TOP OLYMPIAN

In 2016, Biles headed to the Olympics for the first time. She won four gold medals and one bronze medal. Biles returned to the Olympics in 2020, winning two medals. But she pulled out early for mental health reasons. In 2024, she returned to the Olympics and won three gold medals and one silver!

TIMELINE

2013 wins the all-around title at the World Championships

2015 becomes the first woman to win 3 straight world all-around titles

2016 wins 4 gold medals at the Rio Olympics

AWARDS AND HONORS

- 7 Olympic gold medals
- 2 Olympic silver medals
- 2 Olympic bronze medals
- 30 World Championship medals
- Presidential Medal of Freedom
- 41 U.S. Championship medals

COLUMBUS

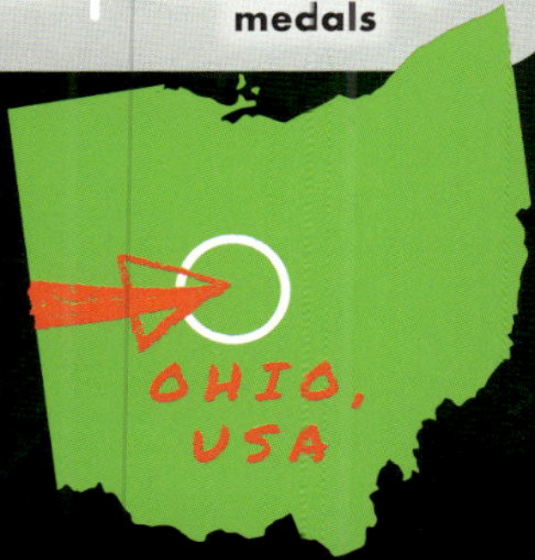

BORN: March 14, 1997, in Columbus, Ohio

EVENTS: floor exercise, balance beam, uneven bars, vault

TEAM: U.S. national team

HELPING OTHERS

Biles works with Friends of the Children, which finds mentors for foster children to help them reach their full potential.

NAMESAKE MOVES

Biles is known for her skill and strength. She is also known for the difficult and creative moves that are named after her.

2019 becomes the first woman to win 5 world all-around titles

2020 wins bronze and silver medals at the Tokyo Olympics

2024 becomes the first gymnast to win 9 all-around titles

Trischa Zorn

Trischa Zorn is a blind swimmer who became the most decorated Paralympian in history. She won dozens of medals in a wide variety of events and helped change how the top Paralympic athletes trained.

BORN BLIND

Zorn was born with an eye condition that left her blind. As a child growing up in California, she loved to swim. When she was 10, she began training with a swim team. At age 16, she competed in the 1980 Paralympic Games for the first time. She won seven gold medals!

BREAKING RECORDS

After high school, Zorn swam for the University of Nebraska. She was the first visually impaired athlete to earn an NCAA Division I Scholarship. She attended the 1984 Paralympic Games, winning six more gold medals. She also began breaking world records. In 1992, she set a record for the 200-meter backstroke with a time of 2 minutes, 31.13 seconds. She continued swimming at every Paralympic Games through 2004. She won 55 medals overall!

AWARDS AND HONORS

- 41 Paralympic gold medals
- 9 Paralympic silver medals
- 5 Paralympic bronze medals
- International Paralympic Hall of Fame
- U.S. Association of Blind Athletes Female Athlete of the Year

TIMELINE

- **1980** wins 7 gold medals at the Paralympic Games
- **1992** wins 10 gold and 2 silver medals at the Paralympic Games
- **1992** sets the world record in the 200-meter backstroke
- **1996** wins 2 gold, 3 silver, and 3 bronze medals at the Paralympic Games
- **2004** wins a bronze medal in her last Paralympic Games
- **2005** graduates from law school

BECOMING A LAWYER

After retiring, Zorn worked as a teacher. Then, she attended law school. Today, she is a lawyer who helps **veterans**.

SWIMMING ROYALTY

Zorn was inducted into the International Paralympic Hall of Fame in 2012 and the U.S. Olympic & Paralympic Hall of Fame in 2022.

BORN: June 1, 1964, in Orange, California

EDUCATION AND TRAINING: University of Nebraska, Indiana University, IU Robert McKinney School of Law

TEAM: U.S. national team

EVENTS: backstroke, breaststroke, butterfly, individual medley, freestyle, freestyle relay, medley relay

GAME CHANGER

Zorn helped start a program that allowed Paralympic athletes to train at the U.S. Olympic Training Center. This helped them get the same resources as other athletes.

THE FUTURE OF SPORTS

People will always enjoy playing and watching sports. New rules and guidelines will develop, and new leagues will emerge. New events may be added to the Olympics, and more sports may be invented. Whatever happens, there will always be top athletes who train hard to set new records.

MORE ATHLETES TODAY AND BEYOND

CALEB WILLIAMS

Caleb Williams is a quarterback who played for Oklahoma University and the University of Southern California. He won the Heisman Trophy in 2022. He was the top draft pick for the 2024 NFL season to start his professional career with the Chicago Bears.

NAOMI GIRMA

Naomi Girma made waves in college when she played for the Stanford Cardinal. Her team won the 2019 Women's College Cup. She was drafted to the San Diego Wave FC in 2022. In 2025, she joined the Chelsea FC.

FRANCES TIAFOE

Frances Tiafoe grew up training at the Junior Tennis Champion Center in Maryland, where his father worked as head of maintenance. He played in his first Grand Slam match at age 17. He has won 3 singles titles as of 2024.

ARISA TREW

In 2024, Arisa Trew became the first female skateboarder to land a 900. Trew was just 14 years old when she landed the difficult trick.

MEGAN CARTER

Megan Carter was the 12th overall pick in the 2024 PWHL draft. She was chosen by the Toronto Sceptres. She is a two-time Hockey East First Team All-Star and two-time New England Division I All-Star.

PAIGE BUECKERS

Paige Bueckers is a rising star in the world of basketball. She spent her college career playing guard for the UConn Huskies, leading her team to win the NCAA championship in 2025. That year, she was drafted to the Dallas Wings.

GLOSSARY

amateur—related to a person who does something for pleasure and not as a job

ambassador—a person sent to represent an organization or country in another place

analyst—a person whose job is to study something in detail

assists—a stat that comes from helping another player score by passing the ball or puck to them

autobiography—a book or other piece of writing about a person's life that is written by that person

discrimination—the act of treating someone unfairly because of race, gender, age, or other differences

draft—a process used to place players on teams; during a draft, teams take turns choosing players.

forward—a position in soccer that involves trying to score or help teammates score goals

Grand Slam—a tennis achievement in which a player wins the Australian Open, French Open, U.S. Open, and Wimbledon

hat tricks—achievements in which a player scores three goals in one game

inducted—added

LGBTQ+—a community of people who identify as something other than heterosexual or the gender they were assigned at birth; LGBTQ+ stands for Lesbian, Gay, Bisexual, Transgender, Queer and other identities.

playoffs—games played after the regular season is over; playoff games determine which teams play in the championship game.

professional—related to athletes who are paid to participate in a sport

quarterback—the player on a football team who leads the offense by starting the plays

recruited—convinced to join

relay—a race in which multiple people work as a team

rookie—a first-year player

sued—brought about legal proceedings to settle a dispute

unanimous—related to a decision to which every person involved agrees

varsity—related to the top team that plays a sport in a high school or college

vault—a gymnastics event in which a gymnast jumps off of a padded platform and performs a move

veterans—people who served in the military

WRITE ABOUT IT!

- Why do many people think Tom Brady is the best football player of all time? **Do you agree or disagree?**

- Many successful athletes spend time and money helping others. If you were an athlete, **what causes would you support?**

- Michelle Kwan never won an Olympic gold medal. But she is still considered the best figure skater in U.S. history. **Why?**

ALSO CHECK OUT

INDEX

Australian Open, 6, 30, 32
Biles, Simone, 40–41
Bolt, Usain, 38–39
Brady, Tom, 8–9
Fédération Internationale de Football Association, 6
French Open, 6, 30, 31, 32
future, 44–45
Grand Slam, 6, 30, 31, 32, 33, 45
Gretzky, Wayne, 26–27
history, 4–5, 6
James, LeBron, 20–21
Jordan, Michael, 24–25
Kwan, Michelle, 36–37
Mahomes, Patrick, 10–11
Major League Baseball, 6, 8, 10, 16, 18
McDavid, Connor, 28–29
Messi, Lionel, 14–15
more athletes today and beyond 44–45
more sports, more athletes, 7
Morgan, Alex, 12–13
Nadal, Rafael, 30–31
National Basketball Association, 6, 20, 24, 25
National Football League, 6, 8, 9, 10, 11, 44
National Hockey League, 6, 26, 27, 28, 29
National Women's Soccer League, 13
Ohtani, Shohei, 18–19
Olympic Games, 4, 5, 6, 7, 13, 22, 25, 30, 32, 34, 36, 37, 39, 40, 43, 44
Paralympic Games, 37, 42, 43
Phelps, Michael, 34–35
Professional Women's Hockey League, 4, 6, 45
quotes, 15, 28, 34
Stanley Cup, 26, 28
Super Bowl, 8, 9, 10
Taurasi, Diana, 22–23
Trout, Mike, 16–17
U.S. Open, 6, 30, 32
U.S. Soccer Federation, 13
Williams, Serena, 32–33
Williams, Venus, 32
Wimbledon, 6, 30, 32
Women's National Basketball Association, 6, 22, 23
World Baseball Classic, 17, 18
World Cup, 13, 14, 15
World Series, 6, 18
Zorn, Trischa, 42–43

The images in this book are reproduced through the courtesy of: All-Pro Reels/ Wikimedia Commons, front cover (Mahomes), pp. 8 (Brady of the New England Patriots), 10 (Mahomes), 11 (Mahomes profile), 28 (McDavid oilers game); Conor P. Fitzgerald, front cover (Ohtani), p. 6 (Witt Jr. bats); Asatur Yesayants, front cover (Biles); Agência Brasil Fotografias/ Wikimedia Commons, p. 3 (Biles); Dorothy Hong, p. 3 (Williams); Erik Drost/ Wikimedia Commons, pp. 3 (James), 12 (Morgan profile); ASSOCIATED PRESS/ AP Images, pp. 4-5 (1932 Olympic Games, main photo); Colohisto/ Wikimedia Commons, p. 4 (1891 - James Naismith); Scewing/ Wikimedia Commons, p. 5 (1920 - American Professional Football Association); John Lent/ AP Images, p. 5 (1949 - NBA is formed); Office of the Governor of Massachusetts/ Wikimedia Commons, p. 5 (2023 - PWHL); ProPhoto1234, p. 6 (Duplantis Pole Vault); Ralph Arvesen/ Wikimedia Commons, p. 7 (Hawk); Brian A. Witkin, p. 7 (Hamilton); Leonard Zhukovsky, pp. 7 (Kim), 31 (Nadal profile), 33 (Williams main photo), 34 (Phelps), 35 (Phelps profile); Mai Grovesp, p. 7 (Korda); OSCAR GONZALEZ FUENTES, pp. 8 (Brady portrait), 30 (Nadal); Anthony Nesmith/ Alamy Stock Photo, p. 8 (New England Patriot fans); Cal Sport Media/ Alamy Stock Photo, pp. 9 (Brady Profile), 11 (Mahomes in AFC Divisional game), 16 (Trout), 45 (Bueckers); Alfred Twu/ Wikimedia Commons, p. 9 (San Mateo); UPI/ Alamy Stock Photo, pp. 9 (Super Bowl star), 18 (Ohtani run, Among the Greats), 19 (Ohtani profile); Adam Schultz/ Wikimedia Commons, p. 10 (Mahomes portrait); Jeff Bukowski, p. 11 (football helmet); Rupak. bhattacharya/ Wikimedia Commons, p. 11 (Tyler Texas); Taylor Vincent/ Wikimedia Commons, p. 12 (Morgan); Marcus Jones, p. 12 (San Dimas); Elsa/ Getty Images, p. 13 (Challenge Cup); Suzanne Plumette, p. 14 (Rosario); Christian Bertrand, p. 14 (Messi); Beto Chagas, p. 15 (soccer ball); Ringo Chiu, p. 15 (Messi); John McCoy/ Icon Sportswire/ Getty Images, p. 17 (Trout profile); Nick Vendetta, p. 17 (Vineland); Megan Briggs/ Getty Images, p. 17 (The Classic Silver Win); Mogami Kariya/ Wikimedia Commons, p. 18 (Ohtani portrait); grey_ and, p. 18 (baseball); amanaimages/ Alamy Stock Photo, p. 19 (Oshu); Jeffrey Hayes/ Wikimedia Commons, p. 19 (Ohtani pitch); Tinseltown, p. 20 (James portrait); Ringo Chiu/ SOPA Images via ZUMA Press Wire/ Alamy Stock Photo, p. 20 (James Lakers game); diebilderwelt/ Alamy Stock Photo, p. 21 (James profile); A.RICARDO, pp. 21 (James jersey 6), 33 (Williams profile), 40 (Biles with medal), 41 (Biles main image), 41 (Biles profile); Sean Pavone, pp. 21 (Akron), 35 (Baltimore); Jesse D. Garrabrant/ NBAE/ Getty Images, p. 22 (Gold Medalist); Stephen Maturen/ Getty Images, p. 23 (Taurasi WNBA Playoffs game); Matt Gush, p. 23 (Glendale); John Mac/ Wikimedia Commons, p. 23 (Taurasi profile); Grindstone Media Group, p. 24 (Jordan portrait); Rich Kane Photography/ Alamy Stock Photo, pp. 24 (Jordan), 25 (Jordan profile); J2XZ13, p. 24 (Air Jordan shoe); ungvar, p. 25 (Brooklyn); Focus On Sport/ Getty Images, p. 26 (Gretsky); Steve Roberts/ Cal Sport Media/ CSM via ZUMA Wire/ AP Images, p. 27 (Gretsky profile); Harold Stiver, p. 27 (Brantford); George Walker IV/ AP Images, p. 28 (McDavid awards); Frank Franklin II/ AP Images, p. 29 (McDavid profile); VisualArtStudio, p. 29 (Richmond Hill); Robert, p. 31 (Manacor, Mallorca); Kathy Hutchins, p. 32 (Williams portrait); PCN Photography/ Alamy Stock Photo, p. 32 (Williams with trophy); Matthew G Eddy, p. 33 (Saginaw); Focus Pix, p. 35 (Phelps with medal); Steven Ferdman/ Everett Collection/ Alamy Stock Photo, p. 36 (Kwan portrait); Joe Rimkus/ KRT/ ABACA/ Alamy Stock Photo, p. 36 (Kwan skating); Tony Marshal/ Alamy Stock Photo, p. 37 (Kwan); Ann Thomas–State/ Wikimedia Commons, p. 37 (Kwan profile); kevin, p. 37 (Torrance); FA2010/ Wikimedia Commons, p. 37 (ice skate); Fernando Frazão/ Agência Brasil/ Wikimedia Commons, p. 38 (Bolt); Petr Toman, pp. 39 (Bolt profile), 39 (Usain Bolt 2016 Summer Olympic Games); Maja Suslin/ Alamy Stock Photo, p. 39 (Sherwood Content); Efren Landaos/ Sipa USA/ Alamy Stock Photo, p. 40 (Biles portrait); Nicholas J Klein, p. 41 (Columbus); Ethan Mito/ Getty Images, p. 43 (Zorn portrait); Davel595, p. 43 (Orange, California); Scott Barbour/ ALLSPORT/ Getty Images, p. 43 (Zorn profile); Justin Tafoya/ Getty Images, p. 43 (Zorn main); Katsumi Kasahara/ AP Images, p. 43 (Game Changer); zieusin, p. 44 (generic baseball); Todd Rosenberg/ Getty Images, p. 44 (Williams); Sipa USA/ Alamy Stock Photo, p. 44 (Girma); Independent Photo Agency/ Alamy Stock Photo, p. 45 (Tiafoe); Anthony Behar/ Sipa USA/ AP Images, p. 45 (Trew); Justin Berl/ NCAA Photos, p. 45 (Carter).